CAREERS THAT COUNT

SEARCH AND RESCUE PILOT

Louise Spilsbury

PowerKiDS press.

New York

Published in 2016 by **The Rosen Publishing Group**
29 East 21st Street, New York, NY 10010

Produced for Rosen by Calcium

Editors for Calcium: Sarah Eason and Jennifer Sanderson
Designer: Emma DeBanks

Picture credits: Cover: Shutterstock: Gail Johnson (top), Monkey Business Images (bottom);
Inside: Dreamstime: Bigknell 24–25, Roberto Caucino 21, Ivan Cholakov 6–7, 8–9, 16–17,
Alessio Furlan 22, Anthony Hathaway 5, 6, 15, Ilfede 20, Irabel8 4, Joyfull 25, William Attard
McCarthy 11, Monkey Business Images 27, Numskyman 18–19, Panmaule 10, Kampee
Patisena 19, Rowfam 26, Alistair Scott 14–15, Anatoly Stojko 22–23, Alessio Viviani 1, 28;
Shutterstock.com: AnnaIA 2, Claffra 12–13, Volt Collection 23.

Cataloging-in-Publication Data
Spilsbury, Louise.
Search and rescue pilot / by Louise Spilsbury.
p. cm. — (Careers that count)
Includes index.
ISBN 978-1-4994-0789-1 (pbk.)
ISBN 978-1-4994-0788-4 (6 pack)
ISBN 978-1-4994-0787-7 (library binding)
1. Search and rescue operations — Juvenile literature.
2. Aeronautics — Relief service — Juvenile literature.
I. Spilsbury, Louise. II. Title.
TL553.8 S65 2016
363.34'81—d23

Manufactured in the United States of America

CPSIA Compliance Information: Batch WS15PK: For Further Information contact Rosen Publishing, New York, New York at 1-800-237-9932

CONTENTS

WHICH CAREERS COUNT?

Careers that count are the ones that make a real difference in other people's lives. Being a police officer, firefighter, or lifeguard are all careers that count because the people who do them save lives. They are the people we turn to in an emergency and they rescue people who are in danger.

Facing Challenges

If you choose to do a job like this, you will face challenges and difficulties. Careers that count can be very dangerous, but the people who do them have the necessary skills to carry out their roles and a strong desire to help other people. When firefighters rush into burning buildings, lifeguards battle against stormy seas to save people, and police officers tackle dangerous criminals, they do these jobs because they get a huge sense of satisfaction from their work. In this book we will look at the work of search and rescue pilots. They are the heroes and heroines who search for and rescue people who are in trouble in **remote** places.

When boats **capsize**, search and rescue pilots fly to the scene to **retrieve** people from the sea.

After a long search, the pilot of this helicopter has found the person in danger and is lifting him to safety.

Careers That Count: A Career for You?

Some people know what job they want to do, but others find it hard to choose. Think about these questions to help you discover which career is right for you.

- Do you want a job in which you can help other people?
- What are you good at? Which activities or subjects **motivate** you the most?
- Which careers are you interested in? Find out as much as you can about them and what they really involve. Reading books like this one is a good way to discover more.

HEROES IN THE SKY

Search and rescue pilots do a tough and dangerous job. They fly airplanes and helicopters over oceans, mountains, woodlands, and other remote places to search for and rescue people. They rescue people at sea who are in boats that are damaged, pilots who have had a plane crash, climbers stranded on mountains, and more. These heroes and heroines in the sky do their jobs in all kinds of weather, day and night, seven days a week.

Search and rescue teams often have to put their lives at risk to help people in trouble.

WHAT MAKES A GREAT SEARCH AND RESCUE PILOT?

Search and rescue pilots are well trained to carry out their important job. As well as skills and experience, great search and rescue pilots also share some important **characteristics**. They are:
- Team players: search and rescue pilots must be able to listen, communicate, and work with many different people.
- Trustworthy: search and rescue pilots are known for their strong sense of **responsibility**.
- Brave: pilots are willing to put their lives on the line for others.

Which of the above do you think is most important and why?

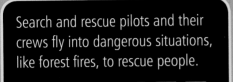

Search and rescue pilots and their crews fly into dangerous situations, like forest fires, to rescue people.

Careers That Count: Becoming a Search and Rescue Pilot

There are some basic requirements that people must meet before they can become a search and rescue pilot. They must be at least 18 years old and have a high school diploma. An undergraduate degree in a field like **aviation** is usually required. People must be fit and have a clean medical record. Those with **criminal records** are usually **excluded** from becoming search and rescue pilots.

A TYPICAL DAY

Search and rescue pilots often do 24-hour **shifts**. No two shifts are the same because the pilots can get a call at any time. When they are not on a mission, this is how pilots may spend their time.

Checking that the aircraft is ready to go and contains all the equipment needed is a vital part of the job.

A SEARCH AND RESCUE PILOT'S DAY

- The day starts with a weather report, which is given by one of the pilots on duty. Pilots and crews also carry out **preflight checks** to ensure that the helicopter or airplane is ready for action.
- Next, crews plan the day's flying training, which usually involves a trip during the day and one at night. When pilots have decided on the type and amount of training they are going to do, they create a **flight plan** and give a **briefing** to tell crews what they are going to do.
- For the rest of the shift, search and rescue pilots do duties such as writing reports and reading new information about their aircraft. They also relax and read, watch television or play video games, prepare and eat their meals, and sleep.
- If the crew is called out on a mission, that job takes priority over everything else.

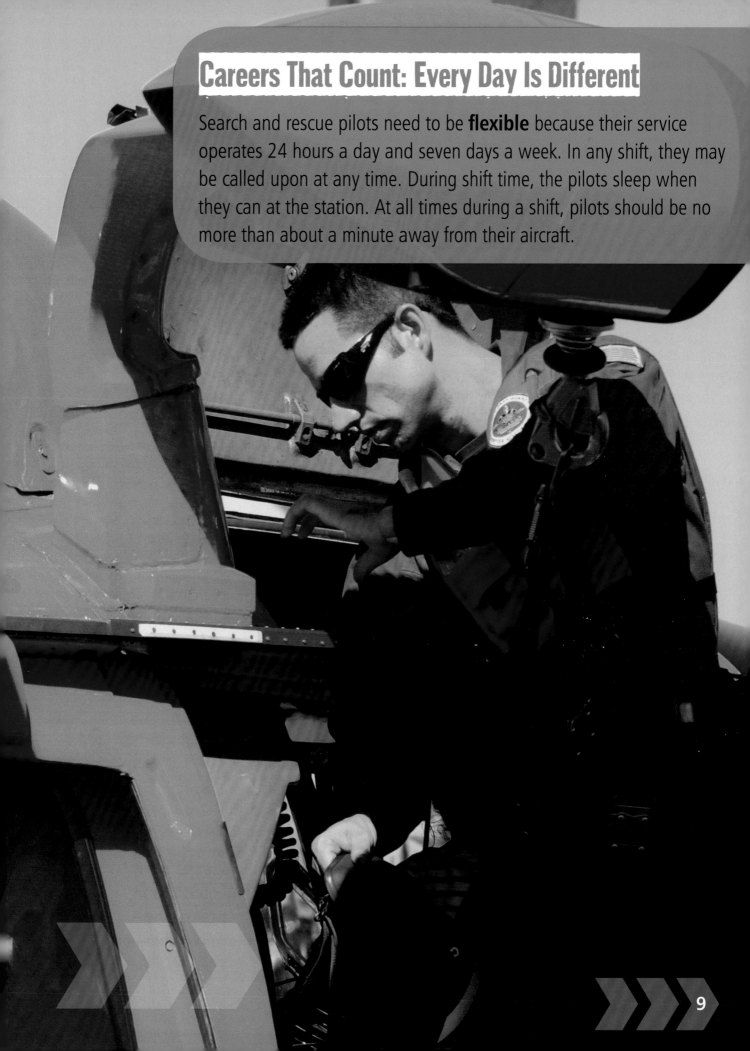

Careers That Count: Every Day Is Different

Search and rescue pilots need to be **flexible** because their service operates 24 hours a day and seven days a week. In any shift, they may be called upon at any time. During shift time, the pilots sleep when they can at the station. At all times during a shift, pilots should be no more than about a minute away from their aircraft.

IN THE HELICOPTER

The search and rescue helicopter is kept fully equipped and ready to fly at a moment's notice. The helicopters are big enough to hold crew, passengers, and all the equipment that might be needed for a rescue.

Search and rescue equipment includes:
- A **life raft** that inflates in water if several people are in trouble at sea.
- A lifting device called a **winch**. This is made up of a long length of cable on an electrically operated boom that can be let out and reeled in quickly.
- A winch rescue **strop**, which are special straps that can lift a single person from either land or sea during a rescue.
- The winch stretcher: this can be lowered from a winch to rescue someone who is injured and cannot be lifted in the strop.

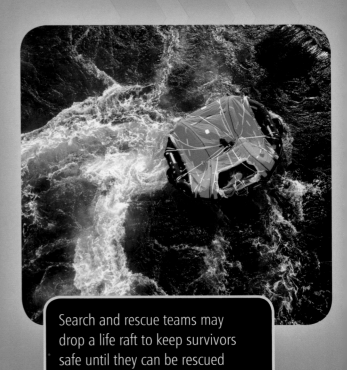

Search and rescue teams may drop a life raft to keep survivors safe until they can be rescued from the sea.

WHAT MAKES A GREAT SEARCH AND RESCUE PILOT?

Great pilots have excellent hand-eye coordination. This is the ability to do things that involve your hands and eyes working quickly and efficiently together, such as catching a speeding ball or threading a needle quickly. How do you think having good hand-eye coordination helps search and rescue pilots?

the winch

winch stretcher

Careers That Count: Flight Controls

Pilots do some training in **flight simulators**. The instruments on the flight control panel in a simulator are the same as those in a real helicopter or airplane. Rescue pilots need to be able to steer their aircraft through narrow or difficult places. Training in a simulator helps them learn how to avoid hard, sudden movements that could be disastrous in a real helicopter or airplane.

THE CREW

In the helicopter, pilots sit in the **cockpit**. This is the **flight deck** area near the front, from which a pilot controls the aircraft. Pilots wear helmets that have a microphone, which they use to communicate with the rest of the crew and with the operations room at the base.

Careers That Count: Navigators

People who help with the flight plan, prepare maps, advise the pilot on which direction to fly, and ensure that all **flight hazards** are avoided are called **navigators**. They may be pilots or non-pilots but they must have search navigation training to meet specific **operational requirements**.

Pilots control the search and rescue aircraft, but they rely on their crew to help them do their job. In a rescue helicopter there is usually a minimum of four crew members: two pilots (one of whom is the captain), a navigator, and a winch person. The navigator helps the pilots know where they are and find where they are going. The navigator often acts as the winch operator at the rescue scene, lowering the winch person from the aircraft to retrieve people who are in trouble.

Search and rescue crews rely on each other to do their jobs.

WHAT MAKES A GREAT SEARCH AND RESCUE PILOT?

The pilot acts as the captain of a search and rescue crew. The crew gives the pilot information such as flight directions, and the pilot makes decisions and gives instructions about the mission. Good communication is vital. Why do you think a pilot must be able to listen to what others are saying and explain information clearly?

SEARCH MISSIONS

Helicopters are ideal for search missions because they can cover large areas of land and land that is difficult to drive over or through. When a call comes in, the pilot immediately begins a high-speed flight to the search area. When the aircraft arrives there, the pilot takes it down to a low **altitude** and flies at a slow speed. This allows the rest of the crew to **scan** the area below.

The pilot can also put the aircraft into **autopilot**. This makes it follow a route without the pilot having to touch the controls, so that he or she can help scan the area, too. To help them in the search, the crew uses equipment such as scanning- and direction-finding equipment. When the crew locates someone, the pilot may then tell rescuers working on the ground where they are.

Search and rescue teams in the air can search areas like thick forest far quicker than people on foot or in land vehicles.

Careers That Count: Spotters

Some search and rescue crews include spotters. Spotters are people who are trained to detect signs and signals that might identify an **incident site.** This helps them locate survivors. Spotters often ride in the backseat of an aircraft and scan the ground from there. They need to have perfect eyesight, with or without glasses.

A spotter looks out for survivors as a rescue helicopter flies over a mountain.

WHAT MAKES A GREAT SEARCH AND RESCUE PILOT?

Search and rescue pilots have navigation equipment in their flight deck and the navigator feeds them information, too. After completing the search in one area, the pilot may have to make a decision very quickly about where to search next, sometimes in difficult circumstances. Why do you think being able to make quick decisions is an important characteristic for a search and rescue pilot?

SEA RESCUE

Sea rescues are needed when sailors are knocked off yachts, fishermen are injured far from land, and boats capsize or are damaged. Once victims have been located, pilots may call for rescue boats, giving them the location of the incident. If this is not possible, the crew lowers the winch person down to the water to retrieve any victims. The pilot holds the aircraft in position while the crew drops equipment, including the strop, life rafts, and pumps that can empty water from boats in distress. They also radio their position and other details to the operations room.

Careers That Count: Swimming to Save Lives

Some helicopter rescue crew members may be trained as rescue swimmers. Rescue swimmers are lowered into the ocean to swim and help survivors who cannot get to a life raft, especially those **incapacitated** by **exposure** to cold water. Rescue swimmers have to be very fit and strong swimmers.

41424   U.S. COAST GUARD

Sometimes it is safer for a helicopter crew to winch victims to safety rather than for the coast guard to rescue them.

WHAT MAKES A GREAT SEARCH AND RESCUE PILOT?

A pilot must be able to work as part of a team. He or she relies on the rest of the crew for directions and information, such as if the end of the aircraft is too close to something. The winch person counts on the pilot to hold the aircraft steady while he or she is lowered on a winch to carry out a rescue. How do you think good teamwork can make a difference on a rescue mission?

RIG RESCUES

Oil rigs are platforms far out at sea that pull up oil from below the ocean floor. Air-sea rescuers are sometimes called to help when aircraft carrying workers from land to a rig crash into the sea. If a worker is injured or there is an explosion at a rig, air-sea rescue teams are called to lift the victims off the rig as quickly as possible.

WHAT MAKES A GREAT SEARCH AND RESCUE PILOT?

If an entire rig has to be evacuated, several pilots and crews must work together. Pilots take turns landing on the helicopter pad and pass on information to each other. This includes details about the height and speed at which they should approach the rig and the **visibility** conditions. Why do you think it is so important that pilots pay close attention to all the small details on a mission?

Rescue helicopters fly over huge areas of ocean, searching for signs of an aircraft crash or survivors. Then they **enact** a sea rescue. When they have to fly to oil rigs, they land on special helicopter landing pads and retrieve the person in need of assistance.

Time spent training in the pool is vital to prepare for real rescues at sea.

helicopter landing pad

Careers That Count: Escape at Sea

Pilots are taught how to free themselves from a helicopter that is underwater using a simulator, in case their aircraft crashes into the sea. They wear life jackets and have an **emergency breathing apparatus**, which gives them extra minutes of air. Once they have escaped from the helicopter, the main risk is **hypothermia**, because the ocean can be freezing cold.

MOUNTAIN MANEUVERS

Mountains can be dangerous places. Avalanches can bury skiers under snow. Climbers can get lost when low clouds suddenly comes in. Walkers can slip and injure themselves. Rescue missions are very challenging in remote and high mountains.

In mountain rescues, pilots may have to fly between narrow spaces or get dangerously close to jagged rocks on a mountainside. Helicopters cannot land on most mountains, so pilots have to hover their helicopter steadily above one spot, while a winch lowers a rescuer and a stretcher or strop to retrieve victims. It is difficult to keep an aircraft steady above a mountain, because winds can cause sudden upward and downward movements. One mistake, and a **blade** or wing could hit the mountainside and the aircraft will spin out of control.

Only the most skilled pilots can maneuver a helicopter in narrow spaces up a windy mountain.

Careers That Count: Medical Training

Pilots and the rest of a search and rescue crew are trained in first aid and other medical skills. This helps them keep people alive until full medical help is available. They also learn how best to move and deal with people who have different injuries, so they can safely lift them in stretchers and strops.

The pilot must hold the helicopter steady during a mountain rescue. One slip and crew and survivors could be injured or killed.

WHAT MAKES A GREAT SEARCH AND RESCUE PILOT?

Search and rescue pilots must be able to stay calm in times of danger. In a mountain rescue, there can be a lot to think about at once, along with the noise of winds and the crew shouting to each other. How do you think staying calm helps a pilot concentrate on controlling the aircraft and mission?

NIGHT RESCUES

Night rescues present extreme challenges, so they are avoided if possible. If a night rescue is necessary, only skilled, experienced pilots can do the job. They need to be able to hover and **maneuver** with very limited visibility.

It is very difficult to search and rescue at night. Pilots and crews wear night vision goggles to help them see. Night vision goggles are binoculars that are strapped to helmets so the pilot's hands are kept free. The goggles work by making any available light stronger. To land, pilots ask people on the ground to shine any lights they have at the area they will try to land on. As they bring the aircraft in to land, pilots gradually change from using night vision goggles to using the helicopter's built-in **floodlights** to light the landing area.

WHAT MAKES A GREAT SEARCH AND RESCUE PILOT?

Pilots work with a lot of technology, including night vision goggles and computers and other digital equipment. The equipment helps pilots and their crew locate survivors, understand wind speeds that affect the helicopter, and figure out speeds and angles of **descent**. Do you think understanding how the equipment works is as important as being a good pilot?

The screen on night vision goggles makes things look green because human eyes are more sensitive to green light.

Careers That Count: Flying in the Dark

Landing in the dark requires a lot of skill. Pilots practice in simulators and in real-life training sessions to make sure they can safely carry out night rescues. They spend hours rehearsing different **scenarios** in different settings to ensure they are prepared for a variety of rescues.

Pilots who carry out search and rescue missions at night have to be very skilled at their jobs.

COMBAT ZONES

Some search and rescue pilots have the job of rescuing soldiers who are in danger. In **combat zones**, pilots may need to rescue a soldier who has been shot and has to get to the hospital, or they may need to rescue a fellow pilot who went down in the sea after his or her plane was hit. These rescues are especially dangerous because they happen in **enemy territory**.

Some of the helicopters that fly into war zones are extremely large. They may have seats for about 30 people and room for 12 stretchers. The body, blades, and **rotors** of these helicopters are built to withstand being hit by bullets and other missiles. They are also designed for extreme **stability** and **precision**, so that badly injured soldiers can be lifted into the helicopter very carefully.

Helicopters play a vital role in wars during fighting and in search and rescue missions.

Careers That Count: Weapons Training

Combat rescue helicopters have weapons. For example, some have machine guns that can be fired out of the doorways from within the cabin. Crew members are trained to use these and other weapons to fight off enemies who try to stop them from landing or taking off.

Making sure a search and rescue helicopter has all the medical and other equipment needed is essential in a war zone.

WHAT MAKES A GREAT SEARCH AND RESCUE PILOT?

Pilots that fly into combat zones may face attack from the ground and the air. They have to stay calm and work to the best of their ability in noisy, frightening situations. How important do you think it is that search and rescue pilots are brave and put the needs of others before their own?

RISKS AND REWARDS

Being a search and rescue pilot has risks. Pilots fly in conditions that all other pilots avoid. They fly at night, in gales, through clouds, driving rain, and in poor visibility. They fly below cliffs, down narrow valleys, and next to steep mountainsides. They also fly above large ships that can suddenly jerk upward on high waves. Why do search and rescue pilots take these risks?

Search and rescue pilots do their job because it is rewarding and satisfying. They are proud that they save people's lives. They understand the risks of the job, but they are highly trained and they work with excellent safety equipment. As a result, there are few **casualties**.

For a search and rescue pilot, it is hard to beat the feeling of rescuing someone and bringing them back to safety.

WHAT MAKES A GREAT SEARCH AND RESCUE PILOT?

Search and rescue pilots not only fly the aircraft, but they also lead the crew. The lives of many people rely on these pilots and the decisions they make. Search and rescue pilots need a cool head and nerves of steel. Do you think you have what it takes to become a search and rescue pilot?

Search and rescue pilots are responsible for the lives of their crew and those they rescue.

Careers That Count: Book Work

Being a pilot is not all about the excitement of flying. Pilots also have to study. They read about the theory of flight, the weather, navigation, and technical information about how aircraft work. Pilots must be intelligent and willing to put in the time to learn this background knowledge.

COULD YOU HAVE A CAREER THAT COUNTS?

Do you want to become a search and rescue pilot? Following these steps will help you reach your goal.

Subjects to study at school: You do not need to study particular subjects, but math, science, engineering, and technology will be useful. Take opportunities to practice teamwork while at school, and to mix and deal with people from a wide range of backgrounds.

Work experience: Get a private pilot's license and gain flying "time" and experience in a helicopter to meet entry-level job requirements.

Exams to pass: You will need to have a high school diploma.

College: An undergraduate degree in a field such as aviation is usually required.

Life experience: Get fit and stay fit. Search and rescue pilots have to pass a fitness check and a medical examination before they will be accepted.

Join the military: If you want to work for the military, you could apply for the small number of flight training slots in the armed forces after you get your college degree. It may improve your chances of getting a place at military flight training school if you already have your private pilot's license, see left.

Getting the job: All pilots must be licensed by the Federal Aviation Administration and pass a written and practical examination. All applicants must provide proof of citizenship, their flight journal, or logbook, proof of pilot school completion, and a photo ID with birth date and signature. Then they can begin the hours of search and rescue training that will lead to their first mission.

GLOSSARY

altitude The height of an object in relation to sea level or ground level.

autopilot A system in which the aircraft can fly itself.

avalanches Snow, ice, and rocks falling suddenly and rapidly down a mountainside.

aviation Flying.

blade A long, narrow, metal arm that spins above a helicopter to make it fly.

briefing A set of instructions about a task.

capsize To overturn in water.

casualties People injured or killed in an accident.

characteristics Features or qualities belonging to a particular person or thing.

cockpit The place in an aircraft where the pilot sits.

combat zones Areas where war or conflict is taking place.

criminal records Records of the crimes a person has committed.

descent The act of moving downward.

emergency breathing apparatus Equipment to help an injured person breathe.

enact To act out or role play.

enemy territory Land that belongs to the enemy or that the enemy has claimed.

excluded Not allowed to take part.

exposure Being affected by something.

flexible Able to change.

flight deck The area in an aircraft where the pilot sits.

flight hazards Conditions or objects that make flying difficult and dangerous.

flight plan A written plan of the route and purpose of a flight.

flight simulators Machines that look like an aircraft's cockpit and that show computer-generated images, which help a pilot train.

floodlights Large, powerful lights.

hypothermia A dangerous condition that happens when a body gets too cold.

incapacitated Unable to do anything.

incident site The scene of an accident or dangerous event.

life raft An inflatable boat used for rescue at sea.

maneuver To move skilfully.

motivate To make someone want to do something.

navigators People who figure out directions.

operational requirements Things needed to complete a task.

precision Exactness or accuracy.

preflight checks Checks completed before a flight.

remote Far away.

responsibility Accountability, taking the burden of something.

retrieve To get something.

rotors The blades that spin together to help a helicopter fly.

scan To look for something quickly but accurately.

scenarios Different things that could happen.

shifts Time periods in which different groups of workers do the same jobs in relay.

stability Not easily changed or likely to change.

strop A strap with its ends fastened together to form a ring.

visibility The distance people can see as determined by light and weather conditions.

winch A hauling or lifting device.

FURTHER READING

Carlson Berne, Emma. *Search and Rescue: Imminent Danger* (Emergency Response). Vero Beach, FL: Rourke Publishing Group, 2014.

Mullins, Matt. *How Does It Fly? Helicopter* (Community Connections: How Does It Fly?). North Mankato, MN: Cherry Lake Publishing, 2013.

Royston, Angela. *Diary of a Pilot.* Portsmouth, NH: Heinemann, 2013.

von Finn, Denny. *HH-60 Pave Hawk Helicopters* (Epic Books: Military Vehicles). Minneapolis, MN: Bellwether Media, 2012.

WEBSITES

INDEX